Caring for an Aging Parent

Honoring as You Serve

Byron Peters

New Growth Press

newgrowthpress.com

New Growth Press, Greensboro, NC 27404
newgrowthpress.com
Copyright © 2020 by Byron Peters

Cover Design: Tom Temple
Interior Design and Typesetting: Gretchen Logterman

ISBN: 978-1-64507-087-0 (Print)
ISBN: 978-1-64507-088-7 (eBook)

Library of Congress Cataloging-in-Publication Data on file

LCCN 2020011245 (print) | LCCN 2020011246 (ebook)

Printed in South Korea

27 26 25 24 23 22 21 20   1 2 3 4 5

In 2002, Mother began showing signs of disorientation and forgetfulness. Her usual spunkiness ebbed away into brooding melancholy or tearful loneliness. The phone calls were confusing and sometimes a bit bruising. Her subsequent Alzheimer's diagnosis began a fifteen-year journey that God used to transform my life and the lives of my wife, children, and siblings.

At first the forgetfulness was manageable. The sadness was more difficult. Anger sometimes flared, but it was hard to know what was happening from day to day, being five hundred miles away. Taking away her car keys (and selling the beloved Cadillac!) was fiercely resisted. Neighbors periodically found her walking—disoriented. I began calling her nightly, and a common conversation could go something like this: "Well, have you looked in the pantry? What about in your closet? Why don't you check the refrigerator? Well, what do you know, you found it! Way to go, Mother! How in the world did your purse climb into the fridge?"

Soon came full-time care (a relative, God bless her). Next, the wheelchair. Then the diapers, the vacuous gaze, the neurological arm-stiffing. By year eight she stopped wandering, and by year twelve she was totally paralyzed and unable to speak.

At that point my sister and I moved her from her home in Kentucky to a nursing home near us. Most evenings I swung by after work, changed and fed her, told her stories of my day, clipped her toenails, or washed her hair. I always ended my visit by brushing her teeth, combing her beautiful white hair, and reciting Psalm 23 to her. Sometimes I think she heard me.

Those were years where I toughened up, learned the art of loving and (at times) firm advocacy, cultivated gospel cheerfulness, and experienced God's unmistakable presence.

Caring for our aging parents is complex and challenging enough when the family is on good terms with one another, no one is an addict, and finances are adequate. But when distance, dementia, depression, disaster, divorce, disintegrated relationships, deteriorating health, and discouragement set in, we may find ourselves having conversations like this with the Lord: "Wait a minute, Lord. This can't be happening. My life is already wall-to-wall busy. I can't manage this. How is this supposed to work with my stepsiblings? Who pays for what? I don't know the first thing about elder care. Dad has never responded well to me—this is going to be a disaster. You know how strained our family relationships are. Moving into this chaos feels like death. I have little hope, fewer resources, my love is cold, and my faith is small. I can't handle this, Lord!"

The good news for the Christian is that, no matter how complex and challenging the situation, God is near to the brokenhearted (Psalm 34:18). Stop and think about that. God, the Creator, Sustainer, Redeemer, and Lord of heaven and earth has made a promise and written it down. In some inconceivable way, the deeper the heartbreak, the nearer he is. It is a ready-made promise for you when you are confronted with a responsibility you feel ill-prepared for amidst the agony of love's impending sunset. It is a promise you can bank on.

I want to offer perspective on two fundamental questions we must ask as we seek to love our aging parents and relatives. First, how does God's Word guide us in this important work? And second, what are some basic, practical issues we need to think about?

God's Word Reminds Us He Is Near to the Brokenhearted

David wrote Psalm 34 during a very difficult period of his life. Saul was stalking him, his family was in danger, and his entire life was pressurized (1 Samuel 15–31).

Yet despite all this, Psalm 34 brims with delight. David calls his readers to magnify the Lord, exalt his name, and celebrate his deliverance (vv. 1–4). God's presence for David is his very food, and he invites his readers to join the feast. "Oh, taste and see that the LORD is good! Blessed is the man who takes refuge in him! . . . [T]hose who fear him have no lack!" (vv. 8–9).

How could David live with such joy under such pressure?

For years I flew about once every three months to spend several days with Mother in her home. Those trips were inconvenient and costly—and I inevitably complained. "Look at all I'm missing! All I'm giving up!"

Upon arrival, the first three hours were frenetic. I bade the caregiver goodbye and jumped into shopping, cleaning, and that nervous "okay, I'm here" banter. I kept checking my phone and wondering, *What am I missing?* But soon I settled in. Cook. Eat (very slowly!). Clean. Take her to the bathroom (very slowly!). Sit. Talk. Be.

Pray. As life slowed down, a quiet simplicity sunk into my soul. I would nap beside her. Sing to her. Hold her hand and tell her about the grandkids.

What happened there?

One tempting interpretation is: a heroic, diligent son set aside his full, busy, and productive life to render selfless aid to his sick and ailing mother. But a more accurate interpretation would be: a son too full of himself was dragged kicking and screaming from his frantic, self-referential life into the presence of Jesus Christ, who is near to the brokenhearted and who saves those who are crushed in spirit.

David's godly realism in Psalm 34 seems custom-made for the challenges and opportunities of caring for aging parents. The pinched schedule ("So many doctor's appointments"), the tense communication ("Wow, my brother has never hung up on me before"), and the growing list of responsibilities ("Dad used to clean the gutters, but no more ladders for him!") are not the defining realities of life. God's presence is. "The LORD is near to the brokenhearted and saves the crushed in spirit" (Psalm 34:18). The more the pressure and heartbreak mount, the more I know "Jesus Christ is near, right here, right now."

Try this experiment: if you've never been to a nursing home, stop by some day after work and visit an old friend or church member. If it's a poorly managed facility, you may be surprised at the sights, sounds, and smells. You may even find yourself asking, "Where are you, Lord?"

Then, commit to keep going. Introduce yourself to the staff, the nursing director, and the activities director.

With their blessing, befriend some residents. Attend their worship services. Hold a hand. Pray. Listen to their stories. You'll begin to notice God's presence. In that sea of broken hearts God is subverting the reign of death through his presence among his people.

The promised nearness of God that David experienced in his hardship is even more lavish for the New Testament Christian. The Holy Spirit has united us to Jesus Christ—branch to vine, bride to husband, child to Father—and "Christ in you" is the measure of his nearness (Colossians 1:27).

God's Word Teaches Us of Our Loved One's Inherent Value

The Bible justifies and insists upon compassionate care—not because our parents are lovable, productive, cheerful, cooperative, or rich, but because they are image-bearers of God (Genesis 1:27) and because God has commanded us to honor them (Deuteronomy 5:16; Exodus 20:12).

After college I spent four months working part time and caring for my granddad in his home. Though he was an exceptionally gentle man, I saw firsthand his episodic frustration and impatience as his mind slowly shut down and his body began to fail. I also came face-to-face with my own selfishness and lack of compassion. "How can getting ready for bed take so *long*? Are you kidding me? Do I have to explain this for the *third time* in three minutes!" As a twenty-two-year-old, taking care of this old guy wasn't always my idea of fun.

Caregiving pushed my buttons. It exposed my idols of efficiency, selfishness, and pride. I found myself tempted to skimp on care because "no one will know"; complain or become impatient because "I'm so tired"; or lash out in anger at others for "not pulling their weight."

One of the most egregious and enduring legacies of sin is the dehumanization of the powerless. The fifth commandment, "Honor your father and your mother, so that you may live long in the land the Lord your God is giving you" (Exodus 20:12, NIV) establishes a timeless principle for caregivers. We who were once dependent upon our parents now find them dependent upon us. The Westminster Larger Catechism specifically applies this principle, directing those with power and authority to be "protecting and providing for them all things necessary for soul and body . . . [not] careless[ly] exposing, or leaving [those under our care] to wrong, temptation, and danger."[1]

God's Word Teaches Us That Biblical Care Is Both Physical and Spiritual

God gifted my grandmother with a sunny temperament and a strong faith. She would say, "I don't get sick—things just happen to me!" Indeed. At age eighty-six she was severely burned in a house fire. Six months and six skin graft operations later she emerged scarred but smiling. Next came cancer. Then the broken collarbone and shingles. The radical mastectomy. Yet a lifetime in Christ, a temperament hardwired for gratitude, and freedom from neurological disease allowed her to keep on smiling. Her cheerful heart was good medicine (Proverbs 17:22). I recall one afternoon, after she had enduring grueling femur surgery at age ninety-six, her coming out from under the anesthesia pained and nauseated. My father, who had been visiting with her, got up to go home and told her goodbye. She looked up at him, smiled, and said, "Well, hasn't it been a nice day!"

On the other hand, Mother's Alzheimer's exerted different sorts of pressures on all of us than Grandmother's injuries. Her challenge was a maddeningly slow neurological disease. You can grit your teeth and bear the third-degree burn, but how do you bear a disease you can't remember you have? And how can the caregiver bear with the loved one who forgets he or she needs care?

The interplay between our physical bodies and the spiritual state of our hearts before the Lord is complex. It's precisely at this intersection of body and soul that a team approach including family members, a Christ-centered church, expert geriatric care, and thoughtful practical helpers will prove most helpful.

Dr. Heidi White, a church friend and geriatric medicine specialist at Duke University Hospital, helped me understand my mother's Alzheimer's not only physically but spiritually:

> Some people get nicer and sweeter with Alzheimer's disease and some people get meaner and uglier—even the most spiritual. What comes out in Alzheimer's is not the bare soul but the

untethered brain, either washing away long-developed constraints on random and impulsive thoughts or washing away lists of grievances long held close to the heart, which destroy relationships. When the person experiencing Alzheimer's "gets nicer," this can be a blessing, allowing relationships to be restored. Or it can be hurtful when they turn vindictive or hateful.

What comes with dementia is not the truth about the soul-state; it is a diseased brain. But God can use even this state to bring healing and wholeness. God may use dementia to open a person to Christian thought for the first time, or it may erase years of close fellowship. No matter the condition, we believe that God knows all and sees all. He will judge.[2]

Mother's cognitive challenges could be somewhat mitigated with medication. Nevertheless, reminding her of the Good Shepherd's presence from Scripture, singing familiar hymns, praying out loud for and with her, and exercising patience and good cheer in her presence were at times the more potent balm. Loving Mother as her Alzheimer's progressed required more (but no less!) than just getting her to doctors' appointments or making sure the bills were paid. We needed to give biblically wise attention to her (and our) *spiritual* condition, even while supporting her in areas where her body was simply failing.

Jesus's own experience of being tempted in all things just as we are, yet without sin (Hebrews 4:15), included both physical challenges (fatigue, pain, deprivation) and spiritual suffering (sorrow, bereavement, betrayal). But think about it—he didn't face those alone. Even though fully God, even filled as he was with the Holy Spirit, he was still helped, supported, and encouraged by a broader community (Matthew 8:1–3; 12:49; John 19:25–27). Similarly, elder care is a team sport, made up of family members, church friends, prayer partners, and financial and medical professionals who can work together for your loved one's physical and spiritual benefit (and your sanity!).

Practical Considerations

Before Aunt Lee died, she told her son Buster that everything he would need was in the blue folder: the will, the funeral service, even down to the dress she was to be buried in. You can imagine Buster's fluster when he couldn't find the blue folder! But it eventually turned up, and the funeral was a celebration of a life well lived.

Sadly, most of us are not like Aunt Lee. We are ill prepared for the practical side of aging. One would think that failing health and the certainty of death would motivate us to get our affairs in order. But only about 42 percent of US adults have a last will and testament, and even fewer have a health care directive.

As we walk alongside our parents as they age, it's helpful to be aware of the representative challenges they face, as well as to be aware of principles that can guide our service.

Normalize "The Conversation"

As our parents transition from independence to dependence, from health to sickness, and perhaps from certainty to fear, we will become responsible for things they used to manage (see 1 Timothy 5:3–5). She used to pay her bills, but now she's writing checks to telemarketers. He used to be a wonderful cook, but now the refrigerator is bare and not a pot has been moved in a week. How can we wisely negotiate these changes?

Bill Crittenden, a geriatric care specialist, encourages us to engage our parents in what he calls "The Conversation." It's really a series of conversations with our loved ones about the transitions they are facing as they age. Crittenden's advice is simple: "You know all those questions you have about how and where your parents will live, who will care for them, how much money they have, where they want to be buried, etc.? They have the same questions. So prayerfully initiate that conversation, with a view toward it becoming a normal, loving, honest and regular conversation.

"Don't approach these conversations as though you have all the answers," Crittenden adds, "but as an interested and curious listener. Often I hear children approach their parents with a sort of ultimatum. 'Okay, Mom, here's what needs to happen. You need to sell the house, get rid of all that junk, and move into . . . ' That probably won't get you very far. A much better approach is to involve your loved ones in these conversations and decisions as they are able. Build trust as you come alongside them, respecting their inherent right (and responsibility) to determine the course of their own lives as long as they are able to do so."[3]

Dr. White agrees. Professionals in her field are increasingly emphasizing the importance of helping our loved ones meet *their* goals. She speaks of the importance of the conversation as well.

> Help your loved ones know they have a safe environment for conversations about their future. Growing old is a lot about change. We all need to cultivate adaptability and learn to accept dependence and help. Christ designed us to not only give but to receive care from others. This can be difficult for older people to accept. Our conversations with them can help break down this fear by letting them know that they are a valued part of the decision-making process.[4]

Dr. White suggests starting with something practical: "Hey Mother, could you show me how you use that nifty daily pill holder of yours? I don't have one of those." That gives you the opportunity to see if she is able to manage her prescriptions. As her capacities begin to fail, ask the doctor if it is okay for you to sit in on her appointments when appropriate. And then, ask *her*: "Mother, would you mind if, after the doctor examines you, I step in so I can hear what she has to say to you? I could even take some notes for us to review together later."

Crittenden suggests wandering into these conversations. Something like: "Hey, Dad, we recently completed our will and some related documents so that, if anything were to happen to us, our assets wouldn't be stuck in the court system for so long. Have you and Mother had the opportunity to get yours done yet?" Or maybe, "Mom, I've just been marveling at how grateful I am that God has given this house to you for all these years. It got me wondering—what are you thinking about where you might want to live if, for some reason, you were unable to stay here? What thoughts might you have on that?"[5]

Don't delay initiating these conversations—yet give your parents time to open up. Many aging adults are hesitant to feel as if they are surrendering their independence or becoming a burden. So commit these conversations to prayer and be gently persistent, trusting God to give you these conversations in his time. If dementia has already set in, open up communication lines with your siblings (those who are willing) and work together to move into the uncertainty one step at a time. Document and communicate well, keep receipts, and be sure that everything you do is done before the eyes of the Lord and others in all purity and righteousness, entirely above board (1 Thessalonians 5:22). And remember, God is near to the brokenhearted—even if it's you.

Help Parents Prepare for Financial, Health, and Residential Realities

The categories of money, health, and living arrangements are fundamental to our well-being and therefore are important areas for the conversation.

Assets and End-of-Life Decisions. Be especially prayerful and thoughtful as the conversation turns to money and end-of-life planning. Involving medical, legal, and financial advisors will enable a more objective assessment and will add important voices to the care team.

Here are three categories of documents we should encourage our parents to prepare ahead of time:

- The last will and testament expresses how assets will be distributed upon one's death.
- Advance directives (or healthcare directives) are documents that express a person's healthcare wishes if he or she is incapacitated. This may include a do-not-resuscitate (DNR) order, if that is his or her preference.
- Powers of attorney (POA) may include healthcare power of attorney (HCPOA) and financial power of attorney. These documents assign to trusted persons the ability to act on one's behalf with legal authority in healthcare and financial matters when one is incapable of doing so oneself. It is wise to separate financial oversight from healthcare surrogacy as a sort of "separation of powers" if possible.

It is hard to overstate the importance of these logistical and financial details. Some of the most vicious family feuds arise over parental assets and end-of-life decisions. Families without these documents often face long and expensive estate settlement issues. This type of advanced legal planning (and a vibrant walk with Christ!) will help bring peace and clarity when life is most tumultuous and uncertain, so that your energy can go toward care rather than navigating conflict.

If there are few assets, financial responsibility for parental care devolves upon the family (1 Timothy 5:4). In cases like this, having had "the conversation" will help you and your siblings begin to prepare and not be blindsided. Resources within and outside of the church exist to help negotiate especially tricky situations, so be like the ant of Proverbs 30:25 and prepare ahead of time.

Long-term health planning. There needs to be a family member who understands the basic health concerns and is prepared to act on the parent's behalf if he or she is unable to make health decisions. It may be wise to separate the financial power of attorney from the healthcare surrogacy as a sort of "separation of powers." Generally the latter is formalized with a Designation of Health Care Surrogate or a healthcare directive form. If at all possible, have this conversation as a family before health fails, so that your parents are able to express their wills and desires. Generally, the surrogate is wise to consult with other trusted family and care-team members, who can add important perspectives if he or she needs to exercise the responsibility as healthcare surrogate.

Long-term residence in case of declining health. Obviously the question of where our parents will reside is a complex one that each family must negotiate. Recent research indicates that keeping the elderly in their own homes is generally a good goal—if it is safe and financially feasible. Often just a few minor changes like wheelchair ramps, handrails, or an easily accessible shower can help our loved ones remain at home longer. Some families are able to bring elderly parents into their own homes. One family in our church had four generations under one roof for years. For them, it worked well. For others, it may not be feasible or desirable. Others opt for assisted living arrangements. Some of these residences are staged, so that as health declines services can be expanded.

In all of this, it is very important to remember that the more dependent your loved one becomes, the more vulnerable he or she is. Nursing or in-home care is only as good as those providing the care. Residents in facilities whose families or friends regularly visit them and occasionally make surprise visits are often better cared for than those who have no interested visitors or advocates.

If your parent is bedridden, learn how to change the sheets (without throwing out your back), check for bedsores, change linens, check hydration, and feed your parent meals. Clean his or her feet, ears, and nose. Check diapers. Take an interest in medications—many patients are overmedicated, rendering them lethargic or disoriented. Report any delinquency up the chain of command. Show kindness to the staff—especially the certified nursing assistants and cleaning staff. One young woman who cared for my mother was so cheerful and diligent that I helped her find a part-time job caring for someone in our church. Your personal interest in their lives and love for them will rebound in blessings to your dependent loved one and may open opportunities for the gospel.

In these important categories of money, healthcare, and residency, involving your parents in the conversation allows everyone to have a voice. Ephesians 4:29 (NIV) is a wonderful reminder: "Do not let any unwholesome talk come out of your mouths, but only what is helpful for building others up according to their needs, that it may benefit those who listen."

Loneliness and Isolation

The elderly are particularly vulnerable to loneliness and isolation. Just consider what it would be like if you were no longer with the spouse you loved, the family and friends who populated your days, the home you tended, or the church community you loved. And if attitudes of pride, unforgiveness, and bitterness have severed relationships, our loved ones may face day after day of disheartening solitude.

In my experience, just a little planning and Spirit-filled cheerfulness can help chase the gloom away.

First, set up a simple visitation schedule among family and friends. Encourage them to be active and attentive. Fluff the pillow, offer some refreshment, check for fall risks, read Scripture or sing hymns, and relive the old stories. And don't forget to involve the grandkids! Talking with, working alongside, and doing life with a grandparent can be one of the most rewarding mentoring relationships (for the kids) and antidepressants (for the grandparents) on earth (see Genesis 48:9). I recently saw an older, retired acquaintance who was internationally recognized in his field for decades. "What are you doing these days?" I asked. Without missing a beat he answered: "Discipling my grandkids." What an investment! We can help our aging parents who love Jesus to disciple our children as well with a bit of intentional planning.

Second, cultivate cheerfulness. Scripture expressly instructs the one who does acts of mercy to do so "with cheerfulness" (Romans 12:8). Your bright countenance, encouraging speech, and Christ-centered conversation and prayers can help them face another day with courage and optimism, leaving little room for loneliness. We should seize the opportunities the Lord gives us to "Strengthen the feeble hands, steady the knees that give way" (Isaiah 35:3, NIV) with the Holy Spirit's fruit of joy. And when appropriate, we can offer direct words of encouragement, like these written by Archibald Alexander in his seventies:

> My aged friends, permit me to counsel you not to give way to despondency, and unprofitable repining at the course of past events. Trust in the Lord, and encourage your hearts to hope in his mercy and faithfulness. Though your earthly comforts and supports are gone, you are heir to an inheritance that will never fade away. Learn to live by faith: no class of people need the supports of faith and hope more than the aged.[6]

The "Four Ds"

Dr. White encourages us to pay attention to the four Ds: dementia, depression, delirium (especially in a hospital situation), and drugs. Persistent sadness, an empty or anxious mood, feelings of hopelessness or sleeping difficulties may indicate depression.[7] Being over-, under-, or wrongly medicated can also profoundly affect your loved one. A basic understanding of these aspects of care will send the message to the doctors that you are engaged and want to be informed. Don't be afraid to ask questions—the doctor works for *you*!

Spiritual Condition

Spiritually speaking, wise love will mean prayerfully conversing with our parents about how they are doing in their relationship with the Lord. For those who have walked many years with the Lord, this will be a sheer delight.

If good patterns of communication have been established between parents and children, topics such as anxiety, guilt, feelings of loss or loneliness, the struggles of chronic pain, and deep regret can be on the table without becoming upsetting or painful. But some of our parents will have no interest in either these conversations or our practical help and counsel. Learning how to keep the relationship while not supporting parental folly and unbelief can be challenging (Romans 12:18). Here is where your team of wise and caring friends can be of great help.

Take an Interest in Your Parents' Expectations Concerning Retirement

J. I. Packer (eighty-seven years old at the time and still going strong), in his 2014 book *Finishing Our*

Course with Joy, has wonderful insights and exhortations for older believers. One of his big emphases is to stay in the game, to run the last lap "flat out," and to grow into that maturity ("ripeness") fitting for an older believer. But Packer also warns that this is not the message most seniors are getting. Rather than "stay engaged!"—the cultural message is "dis-engage!"

> Retirees are admonished, both implicitly and explicitly, to relax, slow down. You are not required to run things anymore, to exercise creativity, or to take risks. Now, at last you can concentrate on having fun . . . and practice self-indulgence up to the limit.
>
> I see this agenda, well meant as it is, as wrongheaded in the extreme. Contrary to a biblical perspective, it prescribes idleness, self-indulgence and irresponsibility as the goal of one's declining years. Having nothing of importance to look forward to will certainly breed a discontented narcissism. It's a recipe for isolating oneself and trivializing one's life.[8]

As his life drew to a close, the apostle Paul modeled "running through the finish line" to Timothy, his spiritual son, "I have fought the good fight, I have finished the course, I have kept the faith." (2 Timothy 4:6). Recently I visited the nursing home after the death of a dear friend who had become my "spiritual mother." As I was breaking the news to other residents, thinking I would be the one doing the comforting, the exact opposite happened.

One resident said, "Like my grandma use to say, 'We born. We die. We gotta be ready.'" Another smiled and said "She made it to heaven before me, that rascal!" Our next worship service at the nursing home dripped with dew from heaven as we remembered Mrs. Scott, opened God's Word, and sang of God's faithfulness through Jesus Christ to the end.

Conclusion

Remember the suffocating fears and doubts we identified as we began this booklet? Caring for an aging parent can seem overwhelming at first. It can break our hearts. But God is near to the brokenhearted. And when God is near, he gives us life, light, power, and direction. Things begin to clear one step at a time.

God is not surprised by what faces you. He has ordained your days, and the "honoring and serving" that is now before you is his good plan for you. Faithfully caring for your aging parents will challenge your idols, wrangle your selfishness, cultivate your cheerfulness, and deepen your dependency upon Christ. Your love will grow. Your compassion will enlarge. Your wisdom will ripen. You'll learn to become a "team player." The next generation will notice and learn from your example. In many ways it is a once-in-a-lifetime opportunity to glorify God and truly love your nearest neighbor for Jesus's sake. It pleases God when you care for your aging parent in the power of the Holy Spirit, attentive to the wisdom of his word, the Bible—honoring as you serve. So "excel still more" in this great privilege (1 Thessalonians 4:1, NASB).

Additional Resources

- A wealth of resources can be found at the National Institute on Aging, https://www.nia.nih.gov/health.

- Every part of the US is covered by an Area Agency on Aging. This is the place to go to learn about area resources both community and facility-based. To find one in your area, see https://eldercare.acl.gov/Public/About/Aging_Network/AAA.aspx.

- The Alzheimer Association provides great guidance on many things, including having difficult conversations. Here is just one example, regarding the dreaded conversation around driving: https://www.alz.org/help-support/caregiving/safety/dementia-driving.

- *Advance directives* refers to official documents related to healthcare decision-making. These documents differ by state. More information can be found at https://www.aarp.org/caregiving/financial-legal/free-printable-advance-directives.

Endnotes

1. The Westminster Larger Catechism, Questions 129 and 130, https://www.apuritansmind.com/westminster-standards/larger-catechism.

2. Heidi White, conversation with the author, June 2014.

3. Bill Crittenden, conversation with the author, November 2019.

4. White, conversation with the author, November 2019.

5. Crittenden, conversation with the author, November 2019.

6. Archibald Alexander, *Aging in Grace: Letters to Those in the Autumn of Life* (Madison, MS: Log College Press, 2018), 9.

7. "Depression and Older Adults," National Institute on Aging, U.S. Department of Health and Human Services, May 1, 2017, https://nia.nih.gov/health/depression-and-older-adults.

8. J. I. Packer, *Finishing Our Course with Joy: Guidance from God for Engaging with Our Aging* (Wheaton, IL: Crossway, 2014), 29–30.